8 MISTAKES MADE BY NEW BUSINESSES THAT **DESTROY** THEIR CHANCES OF BECOMING A SUCCESS

8 MISTAKES MADE BY NEW BUSINESSES THAT **DESTROY** THEIR CHANCES OF **BECOMING A SUCCESS**
(AND 3 TIPS TO HELP YOU GROW YOUR BUSINESS!)

Aaron Loke

Notion Press

Old No. 38, New No. 6
McNichols Road, Chetpet
Chennai - 600 031

First Published by Notion Press 2018
Copyright © Aaron Loke 2018
All Rights Reserved.

ISBN 978-1-64249-063-3

This book has been published with all reasonable efforts taken to make the material error-free after the consent of the author. No part of this book shall be used, reproduced in any manner whatsoever without written permission from the author, except in the case of brief quotations embodied in critical articles and reviews.

The Author of this book is solely responsible and liable for its content including but not limited to the views, representations, descriptions, statements, information, opinions and references ["Content"]. The Content of this book shall not constitute or be construed or deemed to reflect the opinion or expression of the Publisher or Editor. Neither the Publisher nor Editor endorse or approve the Content of this book or guarantee the reliability, accuracy or completeness of the Content published herein and do not make any representations or warranties of any kind, express or implied, including but not limited to the implied warranties of merchantability, fitness for a particular purpose. The Publisher and Editor shall not be liable whatsoever for any errors, omissions, whether such errors or omissions result from negligence, accident, or any other cause or claims for loss or damages of any kind, including without limitation, indirect or consequential loss or damage arising out of use, inability to use, or about the reliability, accuracy or sufficiency of the information contained in this book.

LEGAL DISCLAIMER

Please note, that all information contained inside this eBook is not intended to represent professional business or financial advice. It is not a replacement for guidance from a trained financial advisor or accountant.

This publication – and all information contained inside – is presented to you today for information purposes only. We take no responsibility for any of the information provided here – and while we have done our upmost to ensure that everything is factual, and true – we cannot, and do not make claims regarding the accuracy of the information contained herein.

The information contained herein reflects only the opinion of the author, and is no way to be considered an alternative, or substitute for professional business advice from your trained professionals. If you have financial questions, or legal queries, you should consult with a professional.

The statements inside this book have not been evaluated by trained administrations. The information contained herein is not intended to The Complete Guide to Alternative Cancer Treatments as legal advice in any way, shape, or form.

Furthermore, the contents of this publication are fully protected by international copyright law. Please note, that ANY posting, or distribution of the content found within this book – without prior written consent from the author – will be viewed as a violation of copyright law, and violators will be prosecuted to the full extent permissible under the ruling jurisdiction.

CONTENTS

Introduction	1
Reason #1: A Lack of Planning	3
Reason #2: No USP	6
Reason #3: Time Management	8
Reason #4: No Scalability	10
Reason #5: Not Enough Funding	12
Reason #6: Ignoring The Needs Of Your Customer	16
Reason #7: Not Being Productive	19
Reason #8: Being Afraid To Take Risks	22
3 Tips For New Businesses	24
Tip #1: Get A Good Business Website!	25
Tip #2: Get Your Accounting In Order	28
Tip #3: Brand Your Business!	30
Bonus Tip: Join An International Marketing Company	33

INTRODUCTION

I've worked in business most of my adult life, and if there's one thing I've learned from both running my own businesses, and working with *other* businesses, it's that there are a few main 'mistakes' entrepreneurs make that stops them from getting the levels of success in their business that they deserve.

While it's true that business isn't easy – and certainly isn't for everyone – there is no doubt that a MASSIVE amount of money is available to be made – particularly with the growth of the internet…

And in this eBook, I'm going to reveal to you the top 8 mistakes most businesses and entrepreneurs make, that dooms them to failure.

Make sure you read through the entire book, as I'll offer solutions to these common problems – and I'll also show you a unique opportunity at the end, that will allow YOU to grow a successful business, and make a lot of money.

We're going to begin by looking at – what in my opinion – is possibly the single biggest mistake business owners make…so, without further ado, let's get started!

REASON #1: A LACK OF PLANNING

Most people realize that starting a business requires planning – but almost ALL business owners fail to realize just how much planning actually needs to go into a business to ensure its success.

For example, if you want to be able to compete against your competitors, you need a solid plan in place to ensure that you can offer a better service than that of your competitors – and below, we'll look at three ways in which you CAN successfully plan, for your new business venture.

1. Know Your Market: Knowing how your market – and indeed target audience – thinks, feels, and WANTS, is crucial to you forming a business that's adept and suitable for your target market, and if you're planning a business, you should be planning in accordance with what your market wants. This means that when you're playing your business, you MUST take a look at the market size, the market wants, and more – and this will help you ensure that your business is structured and designed in a way that helps to meet your audiences' needs and requirements.

2. Understand Your Competition: One of the biggest reasons that start-ups and new businesses fail, is the fact that they don't do the correct amount

of research into their competitors. For example, if you were setting up a local eatery, you'd want to know every other restaurant on the street... what types of food and drink they serve... how much they charge... and so on. If you want to make ANY type of impact within your market, it's crucial that you know your competition. How are they evolving in the market you want to enter? How are they attracting customers, with their marketing? What successes and failures have they had in the past, that you can use and leverage to your advantage? Having this type of in-depth knowledge will massively contribute to the success of your business, and is a must-do for any new business entering the playing field for the first time.

3. Do The Math: As with any business, money is right at the very core of what you'll be doing – and if you don't have a solid idea of the businesses finances, you'll never manage to succeed. You'll need to go into your new business venture with a solid idea of the costs involved. For example, if you're purchasing goods to sell – what is the mark-up? How much profit do you stand to make per item? Is there a way this profit margin could be increased? All of these questions you MUST be asking yourself – and doing so can make a massive difference in the profitability of your business!

Now you're probably thinking that all of that sounds like quite a bit of work – and you're right. But here's the thing...

Planning a business can make a HUGE difference to the amount of money that you make – and regardless of whether you've run successful businesses in the past, or if you're brand-new to business and are starting a business for the first time, or you already have established businesses and want to start your next business, you'll find that – by planning – you gain a HUGE advantage when entering your market – so it's well-worth doing thoroughly.

Now, onto the second big mistake new businesses make...

REASON #2: NO USP

A USP – or unique selling point as it's known in its longer form – is the unique "thing" that makes your business stand out from the rest. It's one of the most important things you need to have in your business if you want it to be a success, and without it, you'll be entering an extremely competitive marketplace, with little to no chance of actually becoming a success.

Now, when determining what your USP actually is, you need to think of a few things. For example, if you're opening a local steakhouse, then your USP could be a special type of steak that other businesses similar to yours around you don't offer. If you were running an online marketing services business, that your USP could be the fact that you back up your work by guarantying the results that your clients get.

The exact USP you offer will vary – but it's well-worth thinking about, as if you want your business to become as big of a success as possible, then you'll need this to stand out from the crowd.

It should also be worth pointing out that you don't necessarily have to have just one unique selling point. For example, you could have multiple uniqueness to your business – and when you think about it, this would only help make your business even more attractive to potential clients and customers...

So, make sure you do the research, and think carefully about what your unique selling point should be!

OK, onto the third big mistake that businesses make when first starting for the first time.

REASON #3: TIME MANAGEMENT

Managing the time, you spend when opening your business is very important, as it's the thing that'll allow you to begin actually seeing progress.

Now, you may think that time management apps and the likes are the best way forward – but in this section, I want to share a post with you that was originally posted by the popular business website entrepreneur. You can see the extract below; it gives a valuable insight into time management, and how YOU can begin levering it the best way to grow your business (and avoid failure!)

"The reason time management gadgets and systems don't work is that these systems are designed to manage clock time. Clock time is irrelevant. You don't live in or even have access to clock time. You live in real time, a world in which all time flies when you are having fun or drags when you are doing your taxes.

The good news is that real time is mental. It exists between your ears. You create it. Anything you create, you can manage. It's time to remove any self-sabotage or self-limitation you have around "not having enough time," or today not being "the right time" to start a business or manage your current business properly.

There are only three ways to spend time: thoughts, conversations and actions. Regardless of the type of business you own, your work will be composed of those three items.

As an entrepreneur, you may be frequently interrupted or pulled in different directions. While you cannot eliminate interruptions, you do get a say on how much time you will spend on them and how much time you will spend on the thoughts, conversations and actions that will lead you to success."

As you can see, managing your time is pretty crucial if you want to grow your business the best, and most hassle-free way – and using the tips above, you're on a great path to doing just that!

OK, so onto the fourth mistake I see new businesses making that makes them fail!

REASON #4: NO SCALABILITY

If you're entering business with the sole aim and intention to make just enough money to cover your basic costs of living…

Well, then you should really question why you're going to get into business in the first place, as opposed to just working a regular day job like most people.

Here's the thing:

If you want to start a business, you should ALWAYS have scalability in mind.

What is scalability?

In essence, it's the ability to grow your business as time progresses. For example, one way of scaling would be that – when your cash flow permits – you take on members of staff. This would be on a gradual basis, with, for instance, you employing one member of staff first of all… then two… then three… and so on.

The idea of scaling, is that you continue growing your business as you progress, allowing you to begin earning more money, while also growing the number of clients and customers you have and service.

Of course, scaling a business isn't without it's risks – and it's vital that you scale in a way that suits your business.

A good example of how NOT to scale, would be refusing to take on a member of staff, even though you've got a nice healthy sum of money in the business bank account.

Of course, this works both ways, and you'll want to ensure that you don't hire a new member of staff too early – this would prevent you from growing at a rate that you should be, and could cause you to throw away potential growth that you otherwise could have leveraged to grow your business and earn more money!

To decide when you can scale...well, it's not something you can really predict in advance. Just be sure that each month you're analysing your business, and looking at what needs to be done.

If you find you have a lot of spare tasks – and money – then it could be time to bring in new members of the team, or start additional branches in different cities. You get the idea!

OK, onto the 5th mistake new businesses make...

REASON #5: NOT ENOUGH FUNDING

Something that I tell new business owners ALL THE TIME, is that you don't need much – if any – money to start a business. Heck, what with the invention and popularity of the internet, you can actually start a business from scratch.

(Just think of all the website owners, who begun with nothing. Take the Google founders as an example; Larry Page started building Google from his parent's basement with his brother. They didn't earn much at first – but they now own a billion-dollar company... and arguably one of the world's biggest and most influential!)

Now the Google brothers are an example of one end of the spectrum. While you CAN start a business with nothing – cash wise – there are situations when it's actually greatly beneficial to start a business WITH capital.

For example, if you were planning on opening a business where you have physical stock products – take clothes for example – sure, you could begin small...

But doing so would generally mean you have to pay higher prices from your suppliers (as you'd be buying less items per sale you make), so, if you had more money to begin with, you could actually buy in bulk from your suppliers, thus getting a much lower price, and ensuring that you maximise the profit on each item you sell!

How To Secure Business Funding

Banks lend – but it's not guaranteed. However, one of the bigger benefits of borrowing from a bank, is the pure fact that their interest rates are generally a lot lower than other loan companies...

Which incidentally is the second place you can turn too, for funding. Now, be aware than many loan companies will require you to pay very high amounts of interest – and they'll also usually require you to put down securities on loans (meaning your car or house could be at risk), so it's well-worth taking your time to decide whether a loan is right for you or not. It can get very costly if you don't make your repayments, so always be aware of this before jumping in and taking a loan.

Now, the third and final option is a loan from friends or family. This can seem like the best one to choose – but this has a ton of downsides, and it can often turn relationships sour. You know what they say...

Business and family don't mix – and if your business doesn't do as well as you'd hoped, then you could find yourself owing money to family members that you simply can't afford...

So always be sure to do your research, and make sure you have a solid business plan in place before thinking about taking loans – regardless of where the loan money comes from. Failing to do so could cause you a lot of problems later down the line, so I can't stress this enough...

DO YOUR RESEARCH AND DON'T TAKE OUT A LOAN THAT YOU OR YOUR BUSINESS CANNOT AFFORD!

Now, there's actually an *even better way* to start a business, that *doesn't require funding or start-up capitol...*

And it's all done using something called Joint Ventures.

A Joint Venture is when you basically go into business with someone – and by combining your skillsets, you essentially get a lot more done, in a lot less time.

For example, say you're a voice over artist. Sure, you could go it alone, and provide your clients just with voice over work...

But imagine how much more business you would attract if you partnered up with a video animator, and provided a full, ready-to-use video instead of just the voice over?

This is obviously a very niche example – but it shows you the power of Joint Ventures, and that's not all they're good for, either. Joint Ventures mean you don't need as much (if any) starting capitol, as your partner can help with things you thought you may need to pay for...

And you're also going to have two brains working, instead of one, making it a lot easier to attract business and make money!

Now, you may think that Joint Ventures are worse, because it means you'll make less money...

And yes, while this is true from a linear standpoint, it's worth pointing out that thanks to the fact that you'll be able to grow your business at a much quicker rate – while also providing a more comprehensive service – it's very likely that you'll actually end up earning more money than were you to have gone it alone, taking the 100% profit route.

Hint: If you decide to enter a Joint Venture, ensure to always have a solid legal contract written up, so that both you and your partner have clear goals and expectations on who gets what, and when.

OK, so here's the 6th mistake businesses make...

REASON #6: IGNORING THE NEEDS OF YOUR CUSTOMER

Believe it or not, one of the biggest reasons why new businesses fail, is simply down to one thing:

The companies don't listen to the needs of their customers.

Now, I wanted to show you a very good example of how this could be conquered – and I managed to find a very useful and interesting post from Richard Branson – multi-billionaire, and founder and CEO of Virgin. Below, he talks about the importance of listening to customers – and take a look, because the information below is VERY valuable.

"You learn so much about a business in the months before launch," the Virgin Founder writes in a recent *Daily Monitor* blog. *"But your education really begins on the day that you open the doors to customers."*

The Virgin Hotels team is a shining example of this, he says. *"Since we opened our first Virgin Hotel earlier this year, our team has learned a lot more about what our customers want, what works and what doesn't, and how we can improve."*

Virgin Hotels set out to shake up the hotel industry with the launch of their first hotel in Chicago this year – an industry that has been run the same way for the past century – and offer something "not just different, but better". So how did listening to their first customers impact the business?

Although the intention was never to design a hotel specifically for women – they wanted to create a hotel that was better for everyone – some of the ideas they came up with and the features that they added appealed to women and since the hotel has opened female customers have appreciated the extra wardrobe space, better lighting in the hallways and range of healthier options at mealtimes.

The overall reaction to the Chicago hotel has been positive, with innovations including free WIFI, no cancellation fees and no early check-in or late check-out fees that appeal to all travellers, but the Virgin Hotels team aren't stopping just yet.

Your education really begins on the day that you open the doors to customers.

"The process of refining our ideas will continue for a long time – we're encouraging everyone who stays at the hotel to share their views with us," he adds. "You can never have enough feedback and you can never stop learning."

In January, Richard's wife Joan stopped by the Chicago hotel to check it out and when he dropped in to surprise her, he noticed that she already had a number of notes to share with the staff. "Although her comments were overwhelmingly positive, Joan travels a lot, and her feedback will be very useful for improving our services."

Now do you see how important it is to pay attention to your customers?

If you're struggling to think of ways to do this, consider offering your clients an incentive for answering a few questions. For example, if you have your customers emails, you could send them a questionnaire to complete, in return for giving them a discount. If you own a restaurant, you could offer a free desert to anyone who completes the questionnaire.

Don't be afraid to get creative here. The goal – and the number one point that should be in the back of your mind – is getting your customers opinions...

So, it's well-worth taking the time to do this correctly, as when you do, you could find yourself able to help your customers in ways that you didn't previously known possible.

Hint: When sending an email questionnaire asking for the feedback from your customers, consider creating a funnel. This means that after they complete the questionnaire, they're sent to a sales page. This may sound like a Gorilla Marketing technique – but it can actually be insanely effective, and can really help you to both get feedback that can help you grow your business while also making money – so while it's in n0o means a requirement, it can be well-worth doing, so don't dismiss it too quickly!

OK, let's move onto the seventh mistake I see businesses make!

REASON #7: NOT BEING PRODUCTIVE

You might think this is similar to the previous section on time management – but it's a lot more than just that, and staying productive is a great way of helping your business grow faster – and in a way that suits you.

Let's face it – we all have days where we slouch around with little ambition, and even the thought of work wants to make us crawl into bed and hibernate for months!

Productivity, especially when working online is hugely important to your success, and it will dictate often how much money you earn and how successful you become. During my time as a Kindle publisher, I've had bouts where I found it hard to concentrate and be productive, and I've devised a range of mechanisms that will allow you to increase productivity and stay focused.

BREAK DOWN YOUR TASKS

This tip may seem pretty obvious, but you'd be surprised just how many people I work with who set themselves on big unrealistic task, which is almost impossible to achieve. To avoid this, write down all your tasks you need to complete, and break them down into easy to manage, realistic blocks to help you stay focused and motivated.

PUT YOURSELF OUTSIDE YOUR COMFORT ZONE

A lot of people wait until they feel comfortable before they begin working. Others wait until they feel that they know the market inside out before beginning their project. This is bad for a few reasons. It means you're taking the perfectionists mind frame, which online, is not a good idea.

To see results, you have to take action today, and a lot of the time this means putting yourself outside your comfort zone to allow you to make progress you otherwise would be unlikely to make.

TAKE BREAKS!

Yes. Really! Sometimes your brain has genuinely fizzled out, and you need some time to rewind and rest yourself. Whether it be taking a 30-minute run, having a nap or just sitting in front of the TV, it's OK to take a break now and then! Just make sure that you stick to the break times you set yourself, and then get back to work. You'd be amazed what a little rest and relaxation can do to your mind and mood.

WRITE A TO-DO LIST

When I work, I ALWAYS set a to-do list to help me break up my day and allow me to see exactly what I need to be doing. Try and avoid putting times of when you should be doing specific tasks, as this means any time you accidently go-over or don't quite finish something in time you'll be associating yourself with failure, and this is the exact opposite of the mind-set we want to be achieving for maximum success.

STAY AWAY FROM SOCIAL MEDIA

Okay, so I know this sounds a little cliché, but it's one of the biggest pieces of advice I give any of my students. Social media certainly has its benefits, especially for business, but it also harbours huge potential for time wasting, not to mention jealousy whilst watching other people's lives. Try and stay away from all social media during the work day unless it's required to promote work as it stimulates your brain in the wrong way, and makes you far more likely to stop being productive and just sit back browsing.

DO WHAT WORKS FOR YOU

For some people, listening to loud, raring music helps get them pumped and do a lot of work. For others, classical music sets a relaxing tone and helps them get stuff done. And other people couldn't even comprehend the idea of working with music!

There's no right or wrong way that you should work, it's all about what works for you and what maximises your productivity levels. If you find that taking a 5-minute break every hour helps you come back feeling refreshed and ready to go, do it!

If you decide that playing lough heavy metal rock music boosts your productivity...do it!

Don't let anyone tell you what you should or shouldn't be doing, as the key is to finding a suitable balance that works for you and complements the work you're completing!

REASON #8: BEING AFRAID TO TAKE RISKS

Anyone that tells you results in business are a sure-fire thing, are lying to you.

To put it bluntly...

There's never any guarantees in life – and things happen that are out of your control. You may fall foul to poor health...

Government legislation may change, meaning you can no longer source a product from a certain country, or with higher tax rates applied...

And the point I'm trying to make is this: there's never any sure-things in life, so you MUST be prepared to take risks.

Otherwise – business would be something that everyone could do.

Now, I'm not saying that you have to take big gambles – that's more for gamblers and stock investors – but you DO – if you want to create and build a successful, profitable online business – be prepared to take risks that others won't take.

For example, there may be a new product that you're not sure about. Many people wouldn't want to spend the time or money in getting this new product built – and in marketing it – in case it failed, and didn't make enough sales to cover your costs...

And if YOU take this mental approach, then you'll be massively setting yourself up for failure ion business.

If, however, you DO take risks like this – and that's just one example – there are plenty more for you to see – then you could find yourself business growing larger and quicker than ever before.

In fact, one you develop the risk-taking mindset, then you may well find that not only do you grow your business quicker than you ever thought possible – but also that you're making more money than you ever envisaged was possible.

This is important, as it means that you can grow beyond your initial specs – and while you don't have to take big risks, like putting up a lot of your capital, or other rash decisions, it's very important to be inclined towards taking *some* levels of risk, like investing money back into your business, and this is one of the most important and crucial aspects of business.

3 TIPS FOR NEW BUSINESSES

The mistakes above aren't meant to scare you from entering business – but they're ones that you SHOULD be aware of, particularly if you plan on making your business a success.

It's a good idea to be aware of the risks, however, before you begin working on your business, as without doing so, you could find yourself wasting a lot of time, energy, and money on your business. This is of course something none of us want – but unfortunately it's a fact of life.

So, to help you maximise your chances of succeeding in business (and minimizing the chances of you making one of the successes above), make sure you read through the mistakes thoroughly, and take a look at the solutions I offer in each section.

However, I'm not just going to stop there; in the following section, I'm going to give you some additional things to be aware of, that can massively help you in your way to business success!

TIP #1: GET A GOOD BUSINESS WEBSITE!

The importance of a good website cannot be understated – and in this section, I want to share with you a few basic tips to getting your first website up and running.

Putting together a website is not the easiest task in the world, especially for those who are new to it. The good news is that there are many professionals out there who can give you a helping hand, but there are a couple of things you should take into consideration when making plans to develop your website.

COST

This is a major factor for any business. In recent years the cost of creating and maintaining a website has reduced dramatically but for a small business where the marketing budget might be low it is essential to make sure that the site meets the requirements without breaking the bank. Talk to the web developers about what you need and discuss budgetary constraints with them in advance. There is bound to be middle ground that suits everybody.

SEO

Search engine optimisation is an essential part of putting any website together. People looking for a product or service online will need to be able to find your website, so it needs to have the right design and content to bring them in. Good SEO will lead to business growth as more customers find you.

RESPONSIVE DESIGN

Not everyone clicking on to your website will do so from a desktop or laptop computer. The number of people using smartphones and tablets to access the internet is growing rapidly but not all websites can be viewed easily on these devices. Responsive design will allow the website to detect the type of device used to open the page and will show the mobile, laptop or tablet version accordingly. Do not underestimate this – the number of potential customers out there that want to buy goods and services via their smartphone is increasing and they could be your customers if your site works for them!

SITE SEARCHES

This might sound like a very simple thing and in many ways it is. Most sites will have a search facility but in many cases it is not actually effective. Ensuring that any search facility on your site will lead the customer to exactly what they want is important. If a client tries a search and cannot find something then they will just go somewhere else. A good search facility improves the user-friendliness of the site. Remember that the site is for your customers to use – not you!

SECURITY

Nobody is going to purchase through your website if they believe that their details are not protected. You need to be sure that you have the right security in place so that they will feel confident to come back to you time and time again.

By looking at these major points you can begin to create a website that will work not just for you but for your potential clients too. The right website can help to make or break a company, so it is worth the time spent planning and the investment in the web site in order to get the results that you want. Keep in mind the type of customer you want to attract and let them be your guide as you create your site.

Now, you don't have to hire the best website designer in the world – or be adept at coding yourself – but having a good idea of the above, will ensure that you can get your business' website off to the right start – and it's one thing I advise ALL new businesses to do, when starting out.

TIP #2: GET YOUR ACCOUNTING IN ORDER

Trust me; a TON of businesses have failed due to their internal accounts system being flawed.

Heck, even some of the world's biggest companies have shut down, or faced fines (or even prison sentences) for failing to manage their books correctly...

And if you want to succeed in business, you'll need to ensure that your tax affairs are in order.

Now, to ensure this, I recommend hiring a competent and experienced accountant to work with you. This may not be the cheapest investment you'll ever make – but it's well-worth your time, and it can actually be worth doing financially, as, often-times, accountants will find ways to save you money from the taxman that you wouldn't have initial thought possible.

As a general rule of thumb, you should be keeping all business receipts and invoices – and store these securely, It's a good idea to store two copies; one a hard copy, printed out and stored in a locked filing cabinet. The second can be a digital, copy, although make sure that you store it securely – this is to prevent unwanted third parties from being able to access it. (Encryption is the way forward here, and this can be done using companies like Vera crypt.)

Now, I'm not saying that you have to be super-anal about your business, and tracking every single cent that gets spent.

But really, if you want to cut down stresses, and make your tax return time as easy and simplistic as possible, then you're going to do yourself a big favour by choosing to get your books in order from day one.

Too many times, I've seen companies fail because of this – and a really easy way in which you can start monitoring and handling your books yourself, is using online software.

QuickBooks is a great example of a low-cost and easy-to-use platform ideal for new businesses, and this allows you to keep track of your invoices, see where money is going, and analyse different parts of your business.

It's not the cheapest software in the world, granted, but I recommend you sign up to a service like this, as it'll help you stay organized and ensure things don't go amiss.

TIP #3: BRAND YOUR BUSINESS!

Think of the biggest companies in the world; Google, Facebook, Starbucks, Asda, Tesco...

If there's one thing all of these companies have in common, it's this:

They ALL have a solid branding image.

When you think of these companies, you instantly think of their logo right?

And this is exactly what their branding has done for them. You likely can even recognize these companies just on colours (Blue and white for Facebook, Green, Yellow, Red, Blue, and Green for Google... and so on...) and these businesses have done an expert job in exposing you to their branding through various techniques, such as TV advertising, Social Media adverts, and more.

Now, I'm not saying you have to have a million-dollar branding campaign...

But here are a few affordable, yet effective ways to create a recognizable and strong brand for your business:

Get A Logo: You may think a logo is purely something that customers see when they land on your website, or buy your products – but it's actually a LOT more than that. A logo defines who you are. It allows you to create an image in customers heads when they see your brand name mentioned... and it's a GREAT way to show your company's main message, in a relatively simple way. Now, you can get a great-looking logo from sites like Upwork and Fiverr – and these are both inexpensive ways that you can connect with expert developers in other countries... so it's well-worth doing!

Run Facebook Adverts: If your business is suitable for it, then I highly recommend running Facebook adverts. The shear scope of Facebook means that you can reach more people than ever before – and it's possible (using something called targeting) to make sure your adverts only appear to people who have specific interests... so, for example, if you were a debt consolidation expert in Dallas, Texas, you could make your Facebook adverts shows up ONLY to people living in Dallas, who've searched the internet recently for terms like "debt consolidation." You get the idea. Facebook ads just need to highlight a few core points about your business – and WHY customers should choose you – and you can start running Facebook adverts for as little as $10/day, so it's also an inexpensive way to reach customers, fast!

Be Yourself: This is actually another mistake that many businesses tend to make – and it all comes down to a lack of originality. Sure, you may *think* that you should mimic the success of another big company – but doing so actually means your company's brand voice is getting lost. Try to build your business with YOUR voice – this will help you become recognizable, alongside your logo, and will also act as a sales mechanism to attract new customers.

Now, that's just three branding tips you can use when building your own business – use these techniques alongside the other two techniques I shared with you (while remembering to avoid making the 8 mistakes we talked about earlier), and you'll be on your way to starting a solid business, whether that be an online business, or an offline one.

However, I've got one more thing to share with you today – and this could possible be the single most important lesson you learn about business, so pay close attention!

BONUS TIP: JOIN AN INTERNATIONAL MARKETING COMPANY

OK, so you may have all these ideas about building your own business – and that's great...

But let me ask you a question;

What's your biggest goal?

I'm guessing it's to make a LOT of money right?

And if that's the case, then I want to share a little tip with you that will enable you to earn money a LOT quicker...

And without much of the risk that traditional business carries.

Join an International Marketing Platform

So, what's the benefit of doing so?

Well, the main attraction, is that they *already* have a solid business set up and running. They have spent the years of hard work so that YOU don't have too... and if you choose to join, you'll get all of their experience and expertise, allowing you to go out and start making money right away.

<LINK>Join My Recommended Marketing Platform Here!</LINK>

When you join an international marketing company, you'll be presented with ALL the materials you need – and then, it's just down to you to promote, and cash-in!

If that sounds like something you'd be interested in (and after all, who's *not* interested in making a TON of cash!), then click the link below to learn more!

<LINK>Click Here To Start Earning Money From YOUR Online Business Today!</LINK>

Thanks for reading, and I look forward to helping you progress *your* business career!

Aaron Loke.

www.ingramcontent.com/pod-product-compliance
Lightning Source LLC
Chambersburg PA
CBHW020948180526
45163CB00006B/2369